POTTY

PAINTERS, WRITERS
and other
Barmy Artists

Adam
Sutherland

WAYLAND

Published in paperback in 2016 by Wayland
Copyright © Hodder and Stoughton Limited 2016

Wayland, an imprint of Hachette Children's Group
Part of Hodder & Stoughton
Carmelite House
50 Victoria Embankment
London EC4Y 0DZ

Commissioned by: Debbie Foy
Editors: Julia Adams & Annabel Stones
Design: Rocket Design (East Anglia) Ltd
Illustration: Alex Paterson
Proofreader & Indexer: Susie Brooks

A catalogue for this title is available from the British Library.
709.2'2

10 9 8 7 6 5 4 3 2 1

ISBN: 978 0 7502 8378 6

Printed in England

MIX
Paper from
responsible sources
FSC® C104740
www.fsc.org

An Hachette UK company
www.hachette.co.uk
www.hachettechildrens.co.uk

All illustrations by Shutterstock and Dover Publications; except 14-15, 24-25, 33, 47, 53, 60-61, 70-71, 75, 81, 89.

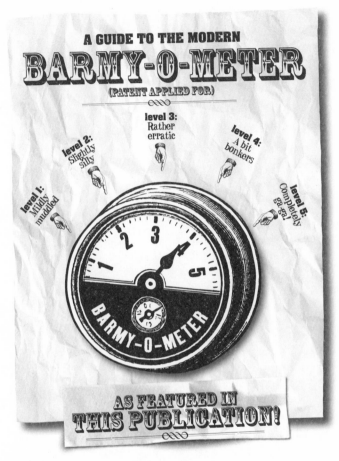

A GUIDE TO THE MODERN

BARMY-O-METER

(PATENT APPLIED FOR)

level 1:
Mildly muddled

level 2:
Slightly silly

level 3:
Rather erratic

level 4:
A bit bonkers

level 5:
Completely ga-ga!

BARMY-O-METER

AS FEATURED IN
THIS PUBLICATION!

How do our Painters, Writers
and other Barmy Artists
rate on the Barmy-O-Meter?

Read on to find out!

THE WORLD'S WEIRDEST
PAINTERS
AND WRITERS
REVEALED

Ever heard the expression tortured artist? It's fair to say that painters and writers have a long and distinguished history of walking on the wild and quirky side. Perhaps it's part of the job description to be, well, individual. But is it really necessary to…

Give up washing? (Yes, we're referring to you, William Burroughs.)

Drink wine out of a human skull? (Thanks, Lord Byron.)

Cut off your own <u>earlobe</u> and give it to someone as a gift? (Come on, van Gogh, have you never heard of music vouchers?)

In this book, we unearth oodles of world-class wackiness and quality kookery from the planet's most famous and well-respected writers and painters.

Keep reading, and you will soon learn about:

👉 The writer who surprised his guests with whoopee cushions on their chairs.

👉 The artist who created masterpieces out of dust and bicycle tyres.

👉 The writer who set up a bed in his favourite pub.

And along the way, we've thrown in some Potty Facts, a selection of Wacky Works of Art and Literature, and even a Crackpot Quiz so you can test your knowledge and show off to your friends.

Turn the page and enter the wonderful world of potty painters, writers & other barmy artists. We guarantee you'll never look at a work of art or literature in the same way ever again!

The painter who threatened his neighbour with a boulder

Sandro Botticelli (1444–1510)

Botticelli (his name means 'little barrel') was the Italian genius who produced some of the greatest artworks of the Renaissance – from *The Adoration of the Magi* (1475) to *The Birth of Venus* (1486). Quite surprising then, that this painter of such grace and beauty once put a boulder on his roof and threatened to crash it through his next-door neighbour's ceiling if he didn't stop making so much noise.

Creak!

Right, that's it! Keep the noise down or else!

The noisy neighbour in question had set up a factory next door and had looms (great big machines for weaving cloth) running day and night. We can only assume that the painter had tried all other methods of bargaining, before hauling a large rock up two flights of stairs. Either way, it seemed to work. The neighbour piped down and Botticelli got back to his painting!

CrackPot Quiz Question

Q. Which animal did Spanish painter Pablo Picasso NOT keep in his Paris flat ...?

a) cat;

b) mouse;

c) monkey.

The answer is he kept all of them! But Picasso (1881-1973) never bothered to feed any of them. The cats had to find food in the street and bring it home for the rest of the zoo.

7

A teller of tall tales

Diego Rivera (1886–1957)

Mexican painter Rivera never let the truth get in the way of a good story. At various times it is said that he claimed: 1) to have been pronounced dead at birth, only to be revived by his grandmother; 2) to have experimented with cannibalism (that's eating people); 3) to have plotted the assassination of the Mexican President. And which of those startling sagas are true? Precisely NONE of them!

What is true about Rivera, though, is his painting ability. His colourful celebrations of workers' rights and the Mexican spirit brought him great fame and fortune. In return, he ate too much (by the 1930s he weighed around 130 kilograms and had given up washing), married the equally famous painter Frida Kahlo, and built himself a model of an Aztec temple to live in.

Rivera's over-the-top dwelling was made of volcanic black stone carved into crazy shapes and filled with ancient Aztec artifacts. Sadly, Rivera died before the house (sorry, temple) was finished, but today it serves as the Diego Rivera Museum. And quite right, too.

POTTY FACTS

Henri Matisse (1869-1954)

Did you know that Matisse's famous brightly coloured collages were done because he was too weak to hold a paintbrush? The great French creator of *The Dance* (1909-1910) underwent surgery for cancer in 1941, and while he was recovering he started cutting out pieces of coloured paper and placing them onto blank canvases for his assistant to pin into place. The work proved so successful that Matisse published a best-selling book, *Jazz*, in 1947.

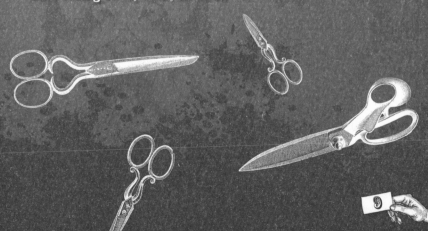

Vincent van Gogh (1853–1890)

Where do you start a story about an artist so, erm, individual as van Gogh? The Dutchman sold just one painting during his lifetime, and painted for only eight years. However, he completed an incredible amount of work (200 paintings over an 18-month period during a stay in southern France) and revolutionised the art world with his powerful and striking canvases.

Van Gogh was fortunate to be painting with a wide range of new vibrant colours, made possible by advances in chemical research. BUT, experts now think it may have been these very colours that led to his erratic mental health. Emerald Green had a concentrated copper/arsenic base and was highly toxic (it was sold as rat poison as well as for painting!). Add that to the lead in the white paint, and the mercury in vermilion, and you've got a highly dangerous

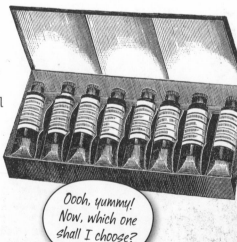

Oooh, yummy! Now, which one shall I choose?

chemical mix. To make matters worse, van Gogh is said to have eaten paint directly from the tube. Yuck!

Van Gogh was every inch the tortured artist. He invited good friend Paul Gauguin to stay at his artist's retreat in Arles, France, but when the pair quarrelled, van Gogh threatened Gauguin with a razor before cutting off his own earlobe (not the whole ear – that would have been daft) and offering it to a local Frenchwoman he was in love with. Mmmm.

Existing on a diet of black coffee, tobacco and a mind-bending alcohol called absinthe, it's not surprising that van Gogh lost control. He ended it all by shooting himself – unfortunately he didn't quite get that right either. He missed his heart, and took two days to die.

BARMY RATING: 4 OUT OF 5

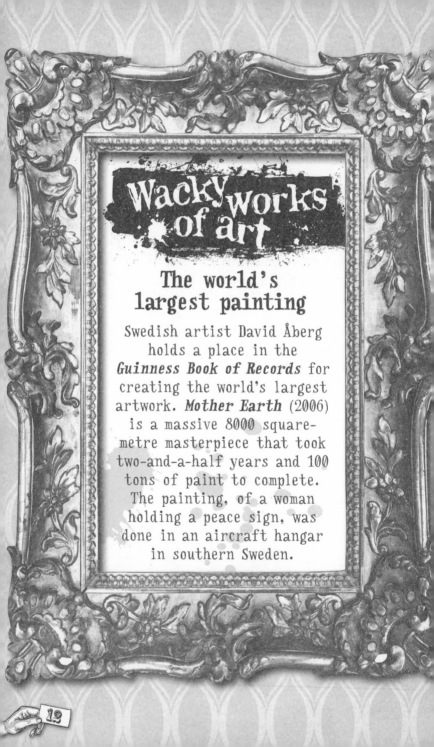

Wacky works of art

The world's largest painting

Swedish artist David Åberg holds a place in the *Guinness Book of Records* for creating the world's largest artwork. *Mother Earth* (2006) is a massive 8000 square-metre masterpiece that took two-and-a-half years and 100 tons of paint to complete. The painting, of a woman holding a peace sign, was done in an aircraft hangar in southern Sweden.

CrackPot Quiz Question

Q. Which writer once said, 'I'm an incredible sausage machine' ...?

   a) Agatha Christie;

   b) Ernest Hemingway;

   c) F Scott Fitzgerald.

The answer is a) Agatha Christie (1890-1976). She was of course referring to her amazing output, rather than the quality of her work (we think!). Christie published an amazing 93 books and 17 plays during her lifetime, which were translated into 103 languages!

Animal magic

Lord Byron (1788–1824)

The famous (or should we say infamous) poet was born for a life of wackiness. His father was known as 'Mad Jack' and no doubt passed on some of his devil-may-care genes to his son. Born George Gordon, Byron inherited his title (and wealth) from his uncle, the first Baron Byron of Rochedale.

Equipped with the funds to support his oddities, Byron got to work on full-time pottiness. By the time he was in his teens, Byron was a certified eccentric who was drinking wine out of old skulls as a party trick. At Cambridge University, he

kept a pet bear in his rooms, and at various times he lived with a crocodile, five peacocks, a heron, a badger, a fox and two monkeys, and always travelled with five cats. Couldn't have been easy.

Byron's death, sadly, was as potty as his life. At the tender age of just 36, he went horseback riding in the rain and contracted a fever. The unfortunate poet was then quite literally bled to death by crackpot doctors who stuck 12 leeches on his forehead to 'draw out' the fever. Of course, what the leeches actually did was drink two litres of his blood, which pushed the poor fellow over the edge. Less than 24 hours later, he was dead.

Dressed for success

Honoré de Balzac (1799–1850)

Well-respected French scribbler Balzac holds the unlikely honour of being probably the FATTEST of the world's great novelists. But that doesn't make the author of *The Human Comedy* potty – no, that would be the fact that he regularly ate dinners that were meant for at least a dozen people (including 12 mutton cutlets, two partridges, a whole duck and 100 oysters in one sitting!).

When he wasn't eating, Balzac attacked writing with the same kind of all-or-nothing approach – sitting at his desk for 15 hours at a time, dressed in a monk's robe, and drinking up to 50 cups of strong black coffee to keep him going. Rumour has it he would often simply chew the coffee beans if he couldn't wait for the coffee to brew.

Perhaps not surprisingly, the French genius produced 97 books, and over 11,000 pages in a 20-year writing period. Unfortunately, it was caffeine poisoning, along with high blood pressure and an enlarged heart, that finally killed the writer at just 51.

POTTY FACTS

Edgar Allan Poe (1809-1849) was afraid of the dark

That's right, the world-famous horror writer once confessed, 'I believe that demons take advantage of the night to mislead the unwary.' Poe's fear of ghosts and ghoulies perhaps isn't surprising when you learn that the author of *The Fall Of The House of Usher* (1839) and *The Raven* (1845) was practically educated in a cemetery! It's true – Poe's classroom backed onto a graveyard and his maths teacher used the dates on graves to test pupils' arithmetic!

The writer who was nuts about tidiness

Charles Dickens (1812–1870)

The 19th-century author of classics including *Bleak House* (1852–53) and *Great Expectations* (1860–61) was a certified clean freak. Friends say Dickens was unable to write in a room until he had positioned the chairs and tables just to his liking. The need to be neat extended to the writer's own appearance – he combed and re-combed his hair hundreds of times every day, even whipping out a hairbrush in the middle of a dinner party if he sensed a strand of hair out of place.

Neat!

You probably won't be surprised to hear that this writing oddball had a few other, shall we say, superstitions. Dickens touched everything three times for luck, counted Friday as his 'lucky day', and always slept with his head facing the North Pole. He believed that aligning with the Earth's magnetic fields helped his creativity. Bizarre!

18

CrackPot
Quiz Question

Q. How did US writer Henry David Thoreau (1817-1862) like to eat ...?

a) with a spoon;

b) with his fingers;

c) with chopsticks.

The answer is b). The author of the acclaimed political treatise *Civil Disobedience* (1849) often shocked friends with his appalling smell, dirty clothes and generally disheveled appearance. Pals who were prepared to ignore that and still invite Thoreau round for a bite to eat were usually treated to the author ignoring his knife and fork and digging in with his (no doubt dirty) fingers!

The writer who never left the house

Emily Dickinson (1830–1886)

We've heard of antisocial, but the respected author of poetry collections including *Wild Nights! Wild Nights!* (1924) took the biscuit. Dickinson went to such lengths to avoid human contact that she often 'visited' people by talking to them through a closed door. When friends came round to see her, she would frequently lock herself in her bedroom, and if she ever saw anyone approaching her house she would run upstairs crying. Even when she was dying, Dickinson would only allow her doctor to examine her from the next room by putting his arm around a half-open door!

Dickinson was also well known for her all-white wardrobe (no one knows why) and was even buried in a white coffin! After her death, she ordered her sister Lavinia to burn all of her 2,000 poems – over 90% of them unpublished in her lifetime. Thankfully, Lavinia thought better of it and prepared the poems (often scribbled on the back of recipe cards or on old scraps of paper) for publication. Well done, Lavinia.

Sob..

POTTY FACTS

Franz Kafka couldn't stop chewing

Quirky Czech writer Franz Kafka (1883-1924) was a self-confessed health nut who worried constantly about his digestion. The author of *The Metamorphosis* (1915), about a man who wakes up and discovers he's changed into a giant insect, followed a diet called Fletcherism. This was invented by a Victorian doctor known as 'the Great Masticator', who argued that followers should chew each mouthful of food 45 times before swallowing it. Kafka's father was so annoyed by his son's constant chewing that he often left the dinner table in disgust.

Wacky Works of Literature

✳ THE WORLD'S MOST DIFFICULT BOOK

Comic novel **Finnegans Wake** (1939) by Irish author James Joyce (1882–1941) is one of the world's most difficult books to finish. Not only is it often written in the author's own invented slang (with made-up words thrown in) but it shifts between dreams and reality, leaving the reader completely confused about what is – or isn't – happening. Nevertheless, it's widely regarded as a classic work of literature. Probably the one that fewest people have read!

POTTY FaCtS

Albrecht Dürer (1471-1528) was Hitler's favourite artist

The 15th-century painter, who is best known for his 1515 woodcut of a rhinoceros (that looks nothing like a rhinoceros) was hailed by the Nazis as 'the most German of Germans'. He was held in such high regard that Hitler himself kept an original print of one of Dürer's works above the fireplace.

During World War Two, many of Dürer's paintings were put in an Austrian salt mine for safe keeping. As Allied troops approached Berlin, Hitler ordered the mine to be demolished, but it was discovered by the Allies and the paintings were saved before anything was damaged.

23

The writer who loved practical jokes

TS Eliot (1888–1965)

The American-born author of groundbreaking poem *The Waste Land* (1922) attended posh Harvard University before moving to London. There he worked for eight years at Lloyd's Bank before giving it up to write full time.

We suspect a serious job at a bank never suited old TS, as his smart exterior hid the heart of a practical joker. He liked nothing better than to surprise guests with whoopee cushions on their chairs, or to hand them an exploding cigar! He even once interrupted a meeting at his book publishers by setting off a bucket of firecrackers under the boardroom table. Kooky.

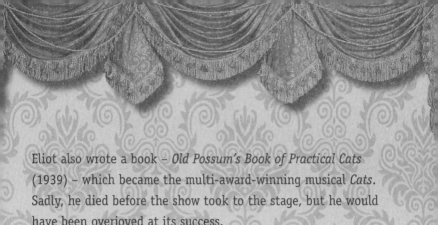

Eliot also wrote a book – *Old Possum's Book of Practical Cats* (1939) – which became the multi-award-winning musical *Cats*. Sadly, he died before the show took to the stage, but he would have been overjoyed at its success.

25

Wacky Works of <u>Literature</u>

✳ THE WORLD'S SHORTEST POEM

Although there is some debate over this particular
award, most critics agree that the shortest poem in
the English language is:

> Fleas
>
> Adam
>
> Had 'em

Sadly, the identity of the genius behind this work is
unknown, but many believe it was the famous US
poet Ogden Nash, who lived and worked
one hundred years ago, at the start of the
20th century.

Crackpot Quiz Question

Q. Which writer was described as 'the laziest boy I ever saw' by one of his classmates ...?

a) Jack Kerouac;

b) William Faulkner;

c) Jean-Paul Sartre.

It was b) William Faulkner (1897-1962), the author of *The Sound and the Fury* (1929) was far from being a model student. He failed to graduate from high school, and got a D grade in English in his first term at college. By the end of his career, he had won two Pulitzer Prizes and the Nobel Prize for Literature!

Lewis Carroll (1832–1898)

To say that the creator of *Alice's Adventures In Wonderland* (1865) was a keen inventor is something of an understatement. His CV includes everything from a tricycle, to an electric pen, to an early version of the board game Scrabble. More relevant to us, though, is Carroll's ability to add new words to the English language.

Thanks to Carroll we now have the words 'chortle' (a combination of chuckle and snort) and 'galumph' (gallop plus triumph). He even invented his own pen name – by taking his real name, Charles Lutwidge Dodgson, swapping the first two words around, translating them into Latin and then translating them back into English. Phew!

Chortle!

DRINK M

his own words

Like Dickens, Carroll was also obsessive about order. Historians say he kept records of dinner party menus and seating arrangements – sometimes for 40 years! And whenever he went on a journey, no matter how far, he painstakingly mapped out the route, estimating exactly how long it would take him to finish each stage, and exactly how much money he would need – for fares, tips, food and so on. Yikes!

Wacky Works of Literature

✳ THE BOOK WITHOUT ANY PUNCTUATION

In 1798, US businessman Timothy Dexter (1748–1806) published an autobiography entitled **A Pickle for the Knowing Ones or Plain Truths in a Homespun Dress** that contained 8,847 words and 33,864 letters – but no punctuation! Despite Dexter's lack of grammar, the book was a bestseller and was reprinted eight times. In the second edition, he helpfully included an extra page containing 13 lines of punctuation marks, which he suggested readers insert where they thought best!

POTTY FACTS

Arthur Conan Doyle
(1859-1930)

The creator of legendary detective Sherlock Holmes
was a huge fan of sports, and excelled at cricket, golf
and skiing. He also loved to box. Nothing potty in that
– until you learn that his usual boxing outfit was a
tuxedo and black tie. We assume he didn't have his name
embroidered on the back of his jacket like boxers do
today. That would have been plain crazy.

No tie today, Arthur?

Mark Twain (1835–1910)

The author of *The Adventures of Tom Sawyer* (1876) and *The Adventures of Huckleberry Fin* (1884) was a colourful character to say the least. Born Samuel Langhorne Clemens, he not only changed his name to Mark Twain, but trademarked the name and incorporated himself as a business.

BARMY RATING: 3 OUT OF 5

Twain's lecture tours, rather than being boring discussions of his books, were actually closer to today's stand-up comedians' acts. One lecture, which included Queen Victoria in the audience, was devoted just to the joys of farting!

The quirky writer had a longstanding love of cigars. From the age of eight, he smoked between 20 and 40 every day, right up to the day he died. He often fell asleep with one clamped between his teeth and surprised friends that he never killed himself and his family in a house fire.

A lifelong lover of cats, Twain went as far as renting kittens from neighbours to have them skittering around his summer house in New Hampshire. 'If man could be crossed with a cat,' he once said, 'it would improve the man, but it would deteriorate the cat.'

With a final stroke of wackiness, Twain successfully predicted the date of his own death. 'I came in with Halley's Comet,' he declared in 1909. 'It is coming again next year, and I expect to go out with it.' Sure enough, the comet came back the following April, and Twain died the next day. Spooky.

Did you hear the one about...

The writer who never wrote a single word

Agatha Christie (1890–1976)

The British mystery writer is in the *Guinness Book of Records* as the best-selling fiction author of all time (nearly four times as many books sold as JK Rowling!). However, Christie never once put pen to paper.

The reason? She suffered from a learning difficulty called dysgraphia, which meant she could not write anything down neatly enough for anyone to be able to read it. So the author of such bestselling murder mysteries as *Murder on the Orient Express* (1934) dictated all her books to a secretary, who typed everything out on her behalf.

Christie killed off more than half of her novels' victims by poisoning. What is just as interesting, and infinitely odder, is that she once chloroformed a hedgehog that had got tangled in her family's tennis net! Don't worry, she wasn't trying to do it harm – chloroform is used to put a patient to sleep. The kindly author then untangled the ball of spikes and set it on its way again.

34

Crackpot Quiz Question

Q. Where did Walt Whitman spend the last 19 years of his life ...?

a) in bed;

b) in Paris;

c) in the bath.

Amazingly, the answer is c). The author of poetry collection *Leaves of Grass* (1855), who inspired everyone from singer Bob Dylan to former US president Ronald Reagan, moved in with his brother in 1873 and spent most of the rest of his life splashing around in the bath singing *The Star-Spangled Banner*. Whitman (1819-1892) didn't even dry himself off when he received a visit from fellow author Oscar Wilde, although he did give the Irish author a big kiss on the lips when he praised *Leaves of Grass!*

The painter who was obsessed with war

Leonardo da Vinci (1452–1519)

There wasn't much that Leonardo da Vinci *couldn't* do. Painting? Yep, here's the *Mona Lisa* (1503-6). Sculpture? Yes indeed.

But did you know that as well as the finer arts, Leonardo fancied himself as a military engineer? Moving from Florence to Milan in 1482, he lent his services to the ruling duke, Ludovico Sforza, and produced designs of everything from a tank and a catapult to an aeroplane and even a flame thrower!

However, instead of commissioning Leonardo to make any of his war-like contraptions, the Duke paid him to paint *The Last Supper* (1495), which still hangs in a convent the Duke renovated.

When he wasn't designing dastardly instruments of war, Leonardo either played musical instruments (he was a talented lutist) or started paintings without finishing them! Fewer than 20 of Leonardo's paintings remain in existence, and many are either damaged or incomplete. But there are over 13,000 pages of notebooks.

← The Last Supper (1495)

POTTY FACTS

Marcel Marceau was a hero of the French resistance

World-famous French mime artist Marceau (1923-2007) grew up during the German occupation of France, and lost his father to the Auschwitz concentration camp. For a man who made his fortune not speaking, he was actually an excellent English speaker who helped out the American army at the end of World War Two. The white-faced mute actually started practising his miming skills to keep children quiet when he was helping smuggle them across the border to neutral Switzerland.

The artist who dug up corpses

Michelangelo Merisi da Caravaggio (1571–1610)

Caravaggio was a rock 'n' roll painter – he insisted on carrying a sword (although it was forbidden for non-army personnel), bought expensive clothes, and was often in trouble with the police. His maddest moment by far came when he was painting *The Raising Of Lazarus* (1609).

The painting shows Jesus bringing Lazarus back to life after three days in the grave. So, in order to get things just right, Caravaggio paid two workmen to dig up a recently buried corpse, and to pose holding the body while he painted them! Overcome by the smell, the two unfortunate assistants dropped the body and tried to leave, before the painter forced them back into position with the point of his sword. Now that's dedication!

CrackPot Quiz Question

Q. What was the name of the writer Gertrude Stein's favourite cat ...?

a) Churchill;

b) Roosevelt;

c) Hitler.

The answer is c) Hitler – because of the animal's black 'moustache' colouring on its face. Despite his name – Hitler was probably one of Gertrude Stein's more normal pets.

Half an hour's work per day is plenty

Gertrude Stein (1874–1946)

The writer of quirky masterpieces *Three Lives* (1909) and *The Autobiography of Alice B Toklas* (1933) had rather unique writing habits, to say the least. Stein refused to learn to type, and instead wrote all her manuscripts out in longhand. She scribbled away at an amazing pace – averaging two pages every five minutes – and often carried on unrelated conversations as she was writing. Once it was written it was written – Stein never looked at it again, let alone corrected it, and rarely wrote for more than half an hour each day.

Perhaps even odder than Stein's writing routine were her political beliefs. She once suggested that Adolf Hitler should be awarded the Nobel Peace Prize for bringing peace to Germany. Unsurprisingly, no one took her up on the idea.

I'll write this line, then I'll put my feet up!

POTTY FACTS

Rembrandt was in love with his own image

Many artists paint the occasional self-portrait – *but more than 80 of them?* Rembrandt Harmenszoon van Rijn (1606-1669) – Rembrandt to his friends and admirers – simply couldn't get enough of himself. During his lifetime, the creator of the huge, brooding *The Night Watch* (1642) painted himself from young to old, hair growing longer, shorter, looking happy, surprised, angry ... you name it, Rembrandt captured it. He even once painted himself as an ancient Greek philosopher!

Bathing is bad

Michelangelo Buonarroti (1475–1564)

We'd all want to shake the hand of the man who spent four years painting the Sistine Chapel in Rome. But be warned, you'd probably be overwhelmed by the whiff! In fact, the acclaimed artist ponged so much that he had trouble finding assistants to work with him. Not surprising, as the team lived together in Michelangelo's small studio and even shared a small single bed. Nice!

Michelangelo believed bathing was bad for his health. What was worse for anyone's health was refusing a direct order from the Pope, which is why Michelangelo – really a sculptor by trade – ended up painting the world's most beautiful ceiling.

One thing he never painted, though, was himself. Michelangelo was an argumentative loudmouth whose opinions often got him into trouble. As a teenager he suffered a badly broken nose (see page 57) and was so self-conscious about his appearance from then on, that he never once tried to capture his own likeness.

It may have been Michelangelo's self-consciousness that affected his sculptures. Undoubtedly talented though he was,

Michelangelo just couldn't sculpt women – all his figures, male and female, looked like men (but with the occasional long hair and breasts added). Historians suspect he was too shy to ever ask a woman to model for him!

Ok, ok, I'm having a bath!

You'll need to put some water in there!

BARMY-O-METER

BARMY RATING: 3 OUT OF 5

The writer who shot his wife

William Burroughs (1914–1997)

The wild and wacky author of *Naked Lunch* (1959) had a very dangerous party trick. He would ask his wife Joan to balance a glass on her head and then he would shoot it off with his .38 calibre pistol. That's until he missed – killing Joan instantly! Amazingly, Burroughs escaped with a two-year suspended sentence for the crime.

Burroughs was extremely intelligent – he even attended the prestigious Harvard University in America – but he just couldn't stay out of trouble. He once cut off the end of his little finger to impress a classmate (again, don't try this at home, kids) and, before he found fame and fortune as a writer, worked a series of manual jobs, including being a rat catcher.

Can't catch me!

Not content with once selling his typewriter in order to pay the rent (which severely reduced his writing output), Burroughs also gave up washing or changing his clothes for a whole year (which severely reduced the number of his friends). Phew!

44

Crackpot Quiz Question

Q. Which of these was a pen name used by Mark Twain ...?

a) Thomas Jefferson Snodgrass;

b) Sergeant Fathom;

c) W Epaminondas Adrastus Blab.

You might not be surprised to hear it was actually all three! Twain (1835-1910) also occasionally wrote under the names Rambler or Josh. Mark Twain was, of course, not the writer's birth name, which was Samuel Langhorne Clemens. Mark Twain is a nautical term meaning 'two fathoms deep'.

The writer who hated his feet

F Scott Fitzgerald (1986–1940)

Francis Scott Fitzgerald lived life to the full. Never one to leave a party first, the author of *The Great Gatsby* (1925) captured the spirit and excitement of the Jazz Age in both his writing and his life. Fitzgerald would try most things at least once – at six years old he ate his entire birthday cake, including candles! But one thing the author drew the line at was bare feet. He had a phobia of feet, and he never let anyone see him with less than shoes and socks on – even at the beach.

Fitzgerald and his wife Zelda were two of the biggest celebrities of their day, and were on every guest list in town. However, they weren't always model guests. At one party for Hollywood film studio boss Samuel Goldwyn, the pair showed up at the door on their hands and knees barking like dogs. At another they showed up in their pyjamas. And at a third, Fitzgerald collected jewellery and watches from all the other guests, saying he was going to do a magic trick – and then boiled them in a pan of tomato soup! Probably not surprising for a man who used to light his cigarettes with US$5 notes.

The writer who loved danger

Ernest Hemingway (1899–1961)

The writer of *A Farewell to Arms* (1929) and *The Old Man and the Sea* (1952) loved getting into scrapes. Papa, as he was known, lived through five wars, four car crashes, and even two plane crashes! As a child, his mum dressed him as a girl and called him Ernestine, and he seemed to spend the rest of his life rebelling against her – spending his time hunting, shooting, fishing and even fighting.

When there was no trouble around, Hemingway went looking for it. At the start of World War One, in 1914, he joined the army as an ambulance driver on the Italian front. In 1918 he was hit with shrapnel in both legs, and it is said that he plugged the holes in his legs with cigarette butts. The emergency treatment seemed to work. He even managed to drag one of his fellow soldiers to safety, and was awarded a medal for his bravery.

Hemingway wasn't the luckiest of travellers. Two plane crashes left him with severe internal injuries, and he was badly burned in an African bushfire. Nevertheless, he lived to tell the tale – that is, until he shot himself in 1961.

Crackpot Quiz Question

Q. What phobia did French painter Paul Cézanne (1839-1906) have ...?

a) fear of birds;

b) fear of being touched;

c) fear of loud noises.

The Post-Impressionist creator of such masterpieces as The Card Players (1894-5) went through life with an increasing fear of b), being touched. He refused to shake hands, and avoided most physical contact. Once, when he was out walking with fellow painter Émile Bernard, Cézanne stumbled and Bernard grabbed his arm to stop him from falling. Cézanne walked away in a fury, shouting, 'I allow no one to touch me! Charming!

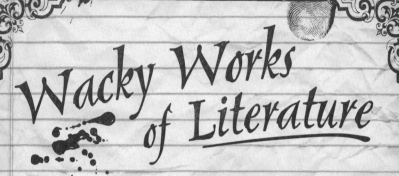

Wacky Works of Literature

✳ THE WORLD'S LONGEST NOVEL

French author Marcel Proust (1871–1922) holds the record for writing the world's longest book with his seven-volume classic *À la Recherche du Temps Perdu* (*Remembrance of Things Past*, if you don't speak French). The book — sorry, books — were published between 1913 and 1927 and contain an amazing 1.5 million words. Ooof.

ZZZZZ...

POTTY FACTS

Jacques-Louis David could hardly speak

The French Neoclassical painter David (1748-1825) who created *Death of Marat* (1793) fought – and lost – a duel when his opponent's blade went into his mouth and straight out through his cheek. Ouch. The resulting wound never healed properly and left David with a swollen cheek that distorted his face and made speaking extremely difficult. Even his closest friends found it hard to understand him.

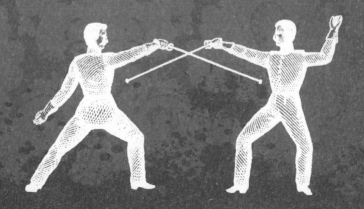

John Everett Millais (1829–1896)

Millais' most famous work, *Ophelia* (1851-2), shows a young woman lying in a stream, with water up to her chin. Being the kind of painter who wanted to make sure he got the details right, Millais asked Dante Gabriel Rossetti's girlfriend, Lizzie Siddal, to pose fully clothed in a bath full of water.

Thoughtful Millais tried to keep the water warm by putting oil lamps under the bath, but it didn't work out quite as well as he'd hoped and Lizzie spent hours lying in cold bath water.

The poor lass caught a terrible cold and when her father threatened to sue, Millais coughed up (see what we did there?) for her medical bills. Still, the painting was the talk of the town when it was shown, which hopefully made Millais, and Lizzie, very happy.

the bath

Wacky works of art

The world's most expensive painting

Frenchman Paul Cézanne currently holds the record for most expensive painting ever sold, when a version of his *The Card Players* (1932) sold for over £160 million in 2011. The painting - one of five in a series - shows two men at a table playing cards and smoking. It was bought by the Qatari Royal Family, who are so rich they will probably buy the other four!

CrackPot Quiz Question

Q. What did writer James Joyce have a phobia of ...?

    a) heights;

    b) thunder;

    c) feet.

The answer is b) thunder. The author of Dubliners (1914) blames his childhood governess (like a nanny/teacher combined) who told the young Joyce that thunderstorms were God getting angry. Even as an adult, Joyce trembled every time he heard the rumble of thunder.

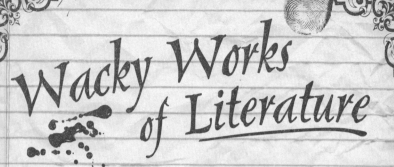

Wacky Works of Literature

✳ THE WORLD'S BEST-SELLING BOOK

British author Charles Dickens tops this chart with **A Tale of Two Cities**, written in 1859, which is believed to have sold more than 200 million copies! The figures are for single-volume books. In other words, trilogies such as **Lord of the Rings** by JRR Tolkein aren't included.

POTTY FACTS

Michelangelo's nose was broken in a fight

As a young man, the great Michelangelo – sculptor, painter and architect (see pages 42-43), liked to poke fun at the lesser skills of his fellow artists. But one day he picked on the wrong guy. Pietro Torrigiano took offence at Michelangelo's teasing and punched him so hard he broke his nose. After that, poor old Michelangelo was, shall we say, no oil painting.

Wacky works of art

The painting that causes fires

Weird though it sounds (well, we did say wacky works of art), a 1950s painting called **The Crying Boy** by Italian artist Bruno Amadio (1911-1981) is believed by some experts to bring its owners bad luck! The painting has been copied many times, and has been found undamaged in the ruins of burned-down houses - particularly across the UK. Spooky.

CrackPot Quiz Question

Q. Which writer once said, 'I could stare at the end of my shoe for eight hours' ...?

a) William Burroughs;

b) JD Salinger;

c) Kurt Vonnegut.

The answer is a) William Burroughs. There's no doubt that the self-styled 'literary outlaw' found the oddest things entertaining (see page 44), but we have no evidence that he *actually* did stare at the end of his shoe for eight hours. Quirky fact: William Burroughs' grandfather invented the calculator!

59

The artist who hated art

Marcel Duchamp (1887–1968)

Frenchman Duchamp liked to offend as many people as he could – usually all at the same time! He started by poking fun at Cubists (who create paintings from a number of geometric shapes, e.g. squares, triangles and so on; some of Picasso's work was Cubist), before deciding to take the mickey out of the whole art world. He created art out of shovels, bicycle wheels, dust and even urinals, and told people he was making them think harder about everyday objects. Get it? Neither do we...

If urinals and bike wheels weren't enough, Duchamp's next trick was drawing a moustache and beard

Voilà!

onto a postcard of the *Mona Lisa*. Then, believe it or not, he created an alter ego – a woman called Rrose (yes, with two 'r's) Sélavy. Rrose – complete with full women's clothing and make-up – created all her own art, and was even given an annual salary with a Paris art dealer to create work just for them. Sadly for Rrose, Duchamp shelved her in 1923 when he announced he was giving up art to play chess full-time. But that's another story.

BARMY RATING: 4 OUT OF 5

The artist who enjoyed landscape gardening

Jackson Pollock (1912–1956)

Pollock was unquestionably one of America's greatest artists, known for his unusual style of 'drip painting'. He was also – for most of his life – an accident waiting to happen. And it often did! Pollock frequently got into trouble. It is said that he once took an axe to a fellow artist's painting, and urinated in the fireplace of a famous art critic during a dinner party. Yeew.

One of Pollock's greatest – and strangest – achievements wasn't on canvas, but on the front lawn of a neighbour's house. Pollock drove his car onto the immaculate green surface one night, and crisscrossed it for hours, destroying the surface and causing £6500 worth of damage. When he was presented with the bill, Pollock offered to go back and sign the lawn, adding, 'Then you can pay me!' The neighbour dropped the charges.

POTTY FACTS

Andy Warhol

The 1960s art icon Warhol, (1928-1987) was shot by one of his fans, Valerie Solanas, and was pronounced dead on arrival at the hospital. Refusing to give up, a doctor cut open Warhol's chest and manually massaged his heart until it started beating again! Warhol recovered but felt the physical effects for the rest of his life.

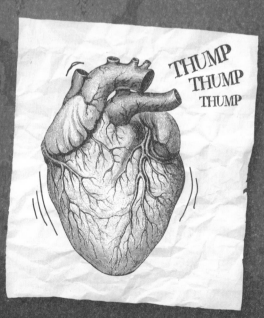

THUMP
THUMP
THUMP

Wacky works of art

The haunted painting

We're not saying that we believe such things … but there is a painting called *The Hands Resist Him* (1972), by artist Bill Stoneham (born 1947), which many people believe to be haunted. Stoneham's painting, showing a boy and a life-size female doll standing in front of a window, was put up for sale on auction website eBay in 2000 with a warning that the character often 'came to life' and walked out of the painting. Even more surprisingly, the price then rocketed from £130 to £672! The painting is now in a gallery in Michigan, USA.

POTTY FACTS

The deaf leading the blind

Irish author James Joyce suffered from terrible eyesight all his life. He wore ultra-thick glasses and had 11 eye operations for everything from glaucoma to cataracts. When he was writing his final novel, *Finnegans Wake* (1939), he was nearly blind and had to dictate it to his friend and fellow author Samuel Beckett. Unfortunately, Beckett was nearly deaf. During one session, Joyce heard a knock at the door and shouted, 'Come in!' Beckett dutifully wrote the words into the manuscript. When Joyce read it back later, he liked the phrase and decided to leave it in the finished book!

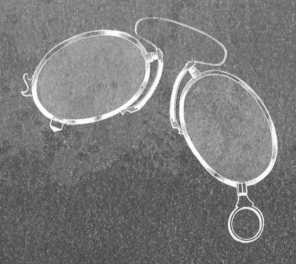

Wacky Works of Literature

In 1665, British scientist Robert Hooke released a book called **Micrographia**, which was a collection of drawings of what he could see through a microscope. Though it might not sound very exciting today, Hooke's book of drawings of plant cells and fleas — on impressive foldout pages — was a roaring bestseller at the time and even popularised the biological term 'cell'.

CrackPot
Quiz Question

Q. What item of safety clothing is writer Franz Kafka credited with inventing ...?

a) the hard hat;

b) the bulletproof vest;

c) the steel-toecap shoe.

It's a) the hard hat. Strange though it sounds, Kafka (see page 21) spent his younger days working for an insurance company in Prague, where he specialised in workers' injuries. For his work on introducing the first civilian safety helmet, Kafka was awarded a gold medal by the American Safety Society. Which we never even knew existed.

Mother knows best

James McNeill Whistler (1834–1903)

US-born Whistler spent some of his childhood in Russia as his engineer dad, George Washington Whistler, was invited to help build the St Petersburg-to-Moscow railway. The harsh Russian winters didn't agree with fragile young James, and he spent much of his time in England, before being sent back to America for army training at the prestigious West Point military academy. After failing miserably to make the grade as a soldier, Whistler hotfooted it back to Europe to train as an artist. Followed swiftly by his mother.

Mrs W moved into a house more accustomed to all-night parties, but mother and son seemed to have got along famously. She organised his social life, inviting his friends over for dinner and even lecturing them on the evils of alcohol!

Er, no drinking boys!

POTTY FACTS

Edvard Munch was a secret hoarder

The Norwegian-born painter of *The Scream* (1893) kept a secret stash of paintings in the attic! After his death, family members entered the forbidden space and found 1,000 paintings, over 4,000 drawings, 15,000 prints, and hundreds more lithographs, etchings and woodcuts, not to mention endless piles of photographs and diaries. In his will, Munch (1863-1944), left everything to the city of Oslo, who opened a Munch museum in 1963. So at least they got them all out of the house...

Aaaargh!

Salvador Dalí (1904–1989)

Where do we start with Dalí? As a child, it said that he refused to use the loo, and at school, he was expelled for refusing to take an exam because he said none of his teachers were clever enough to mark his paper! When he met his wife-to-be, Gala, he tried to impress her by wearing aftershave made of cow dung. So far, so potty.

Dalí and Gala lived the life of celebrity eccentrics, and moved to the United States in 1940. Not surprisingly, they ended up in Hollywood, where Dalí helped create film sets, as well as designing jewellery and furnishings (including a phone that looked like a lobster, and a sofa in the shape of a pair of lips).

Dalí and his wife were in great demand as dinner party guests, and on the celebrity lecture circuit. Dalí never let his audience down. He arrived at one speaking engagement in London in a white Rolls-Royce filled with cauliflowers. At another he entered the room in an old-fashioned deep-sea diving suit and nearly suffocated as he had forgotten to switch on the oxygen

BARMY RATING: 5 OUT OF 5

supply. The audience thought his frantic arm-waving was part of the show, until two stagehands rushed on and unscrewed the air-tight helmet. His entrance nearly turned into an exit!

Ga-ga

The writer who stole other people's clothes

HG Wells (1866–1946)

This son of a professional cricketer failed in fashion, teaching and chemistry before succeeding at literature. Beginning with *The Time Machine* in 1895, Wells wrote dozens of novels and short stories that blended fantasy and science, and predicted everything from nuclear war and genetic manipulation to videotapes and air conditioning.

When he wasn't taking people's breath away with his predictions, however, it appears that Wells was making off with their clothes! After a party in Cambridge, the writer went home with another man's hat. He liked it so much, he decided to keep it and wrote to the owner (whose address was written inside the hat's brim); 'I stole your hat. I like your hat. I shall keep your hat. Whenever I look inside it I shall think of you... I take off your hat to you!'

POTTY FACTS

Edgar Degas was obsessed with photography

Great Impressionist painter Degas (1834-1917) would bore guests rigid at his dinner parties by insisting they sit still as statues while he ran around the room, altering lights and changing reflectors in order to capture their likeness with a new-fangled 'camera' device. And it wasn't just a case of saying cheese – guests had to keep their poses for two whole minutes while the picture was taken. One invite was usually enough – very few guests agreed to a second visit.

Say cheese!

JRR Tolkien (1892–1973)

OK, we know this sounds bizarre, but the writer who invented Middle Earth and sold more than 100 million copies of the *Lord of the Rings* trilogy admitted it himself, 'I am in fact a Hobbit (in all but size).' No, he didn't have excessively hairy toes (as far as we know), but he did have many other Hobbit traits, including smoking a pipe, wearing waistcoats and eating mushrooms.

Tolkien was a super-brainy Oxford University professor who obsessed over languages. He learned everything from Latin, French and German to Old Norse, Middle English, Finnish and Italian. And when he found himself at a loose end, he even invented his own languages – 14 new ones to be precise, with complete alphabets for each of them!

If there was one thing that Tolkien wasn't good at, it was driving. He often drove straight at oncoming cars to try and get them to swerve out of the way ('Charge 'em and they scatter,' he used to shout), and completely ignored one-way streets. His wife was so scared that she refused to get in the car with him behind the wheel. Luckily for her – and for other drivers in Oxford – Tolkien gave up driving altogether at the start of World War Two. Phew.

he was a Hobbit

The painter who used toilet roll instead of canvas

Sir Stanley Spencer (1891–1959)

Sir Stanley Spencer was an English painter best known for his depiction of scenes from the Bible – which he usually set in his home village of Cookham, Berkshire. *The Resurrection, Cookham* (1924-7) shows Jesus in the village graveyard bringing the dead back to life. If that's not oddball enough for you, bear in mind that Spencer did most of his sketching on toilet rolls – they were cheap, and very loooong.

Spencer could usually be found pushing a pram around his beloved village, reserved not for his newborn baby but for his brushes, paint and canvases – he thought the pram's hood was the perfect way to keep his equipment dry in the event of a downpour. His paintings today are worth around £1m each, so maybe it wasn't such a crazy idea after all!

POTTY FACTS

Thomas Gainsborough painted with extra-long brushes

The English 18th-century painter of the famous *Blue Boy* (1770) went to extraordinary lengths (see what we did there?) to create the most accurate representations possible of his subjects. Nearly two metres to be exact. Yes, weird though it might sound, Gainsborough (1727-1788) liked to place his easel next to the sitter, and paint from two metres away – with the canvas as far away from him as the subject of his painting.

When he switched to painting nature, Gainsborough had other wacky methods of getting it right. Rather than stand in a field and paint, he often created miniature 'landscapes' in his studio made of coal (for rocks), bits of glass (to represent streams) and even broccoli (for the trees).

The barefoot writer

Jack Kerouac (1922–1969)

Born Jean-Louis Lebris de Kerouac, this French-Canadian author of *On The Road* (1957) couldn't speak a word of English until he was five or six, and didn't master the language until his teens. Which makes his 175,000-word epic – written, he claimed, in just three weeks – a particularly impressive achievement.

Ahem, your nightcap sir...

Kerouac was the hero of the 'Beat Generation' – post-World War Two men and women who distrusted authority and lived life by their own rules. And Kerouac certainly did that! He moved to the small town of Northport on Long Island in 1958 – with his mother – and was often seen walking barefoot around town pulling a grocery trolley. He set up a bed in the local bar for when he fancied 40 winks, and although he often visited the town library he refused to step inside – and insisted that the librarian brought books out to him, while he sat and read them on a park bench.

CrackPot
Quiz Question

Q. How old was the sculptor Auguste Rodin when he got married ...?

 a) 77;

 b) 67;

 c) 57.

The answer is a). Rodin (1840-1917) married his long-term partner, Rose Beuret, in January 1917 – just two weeks before she died! She had lived with the French sculptor for 53 years. Now that's what we call a long engagement.

Oscar Wilde (1854–1900)

Oscar Wilde spent most of his childhood dressed as a girl. And it wasn't even his decision! Wilde's mother, Lady Jane, was an eccentric poet and regarded the young Oscar as a dress-up companion, pretending he was a girl and fitting him out in a series of elaborate Victorian dresses.

As you might expect, given such an extraordinary childhood, Wilde was a flamboyant young man, who preferred interior decorating to sport. He filled his college rooms with peacock feathers, lilies and blue china, and was once dunked in the river Cherwell by fellow students for his 'odd' behaviour.

It's amazing that the author of *The Picture of Dorian Gray* (1890) and *The Importance of Being Earnest* (1895) ever managed to put pen to paper, considering his self-confessed dislike of work. 'I was working on … one of my poems all the morning and took out a comma,' he once declared. 'In the afternoon, I put it back again.'

Wilde was well known for his wit, which was as sparkling as his teeth were black and rotten. As a teenager, he had been prescribed a mercury treatment by a doctor, which completely ruines his gnashers. Throughout his adult life, Wilde liked to deliver his words of wisdom with one hand covering his mouth to hide his horrible teeth.

interior decorating

BARMY RATING: 2 OUT OF 5

Who's mummy's darling little girl then?

...Er, me?

CrackPot Quiz Question

Q. What job did the writer Jean-Paul Sartre do during World War Two ...?

a) journalist;

b) weatherman;

c) taxi driver.

Answer b). Surprisingly, the existential novelist Sartre (1905-1980) worked as a weatherman (or meteorologist) for the French Army. Existentialism is a philosophical idea that puts every person in charge of their own destiny, rather than relying on religion or government to look after us.

POTTY FACTS

Frida Kahlo treated her husband like a baby

Kahlo (1907-1954) met her husband Diego Rivera (see page 8) when he was painting a mural at her school (yes, there was a big age gap). Many years later, when Rivera was seriously overweight and strenuously avoided bathing, Kahlo would tempt him into the tub with a bath full of children's toys. Once in there, she would happily scrub his back for him. That's true love.

Bath's ready darling!

The world's first graffiti artist

Jan van Eyck (1390–1441)

OK, so the Dutch creator of *The Arnolfini Portrait* (1434) didn't exactly carry a can of spray paint in his robes, but he did create the world's first 'graffiti tag' when he craftily positioned the words 'Jan van Eyck was here. 1434' on his oil-on-oak masterpiece, which depicts Italian merchant Giovanni Arnolfini and a young pregnant woman, presumably his wife.

Being a clever clogs, this groundbreaking artist wrote his inscription in Latin. Neverthless it is one of the first artists' signatures in history, and van Eyck continued the practice from then until his death, with some paintings even claiming 'Jan van Eyck made me'. This one small gesture has launched a million artworks – and badly sprayed train tunnels – ever since.

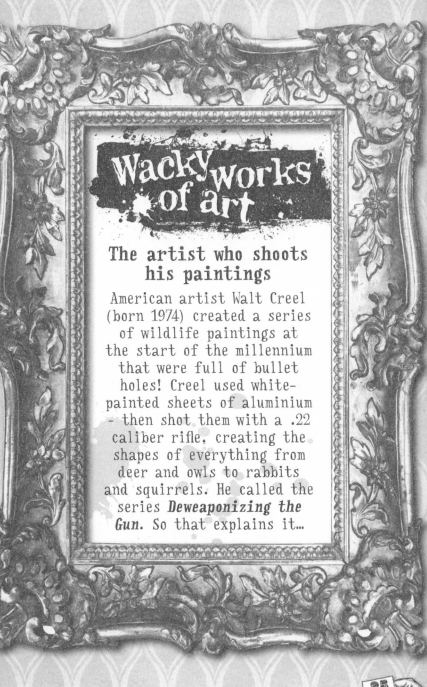

Wacky works of art

The artist who shoots his paintings

American artist Walt Creel (born 1974) created a series of wildlife paintings at the start of the millennium that were full of bullet holes! Creel used white-painted sheets of aluminium – then shot them with a .22 caliber rifle, creating the shapes of everything from deer and owls to rabbits and squirrels. He called the series *Deweaponizing the Gun*. So that explains it...

Wacky Works of Literature

✳ THE BEST-SELLING WRITER WHO NO-ONE'S HEARD OF

Around five billion copies of **Quotations from Chairman Mao** (1964–1976) were published during the Chinese party leader's heyday. Now it's suspected that the quotes of the cultural revolution's leader weren't actually written by Mao Zedong, but penned by his secretary Hu Qiaomu. In fact, rumours have grown so strong that Chinese leaders have had to go on record to defend the book. Mr Hu, however, has admitted that he learned his own writing style from the Chairman. So who knows?

CrackPot Quiz Question

Q. Which artist spent time in prison for fraud ...?

a) Henri Rousseau;

b) Pablo Picasso;

c) Salvador Dalí.

It was a) Rousseau (1844-1910). After leaving school he took a job at a lawyer's office, where he apparently stole cash and a large amount of stamps. He spent some time in prison, then applied to join the army in order to get his sentence shortened. Many years later, he was in court again for a case of bank fraud – using a false name to try and cash cheques. Naughty boy!

The writer who saw fairies at the end of the garden

Arthur Conan Doyle (1859–1930)

Unusually for a man who trained as a doctor before turning to writing full time, the creator of Sherlock Holmes had a very unscientific belief in fairies. He even wrote a non-fiction book on the subject, *The Coming of the Fairies* (1922), based on two English girls who claimed to have befriended a group of tiny, winged fairies at the bottom of their garden. All nonsense of course, but Conan Doyle fell for it hook, line and sinker.

The former doctor was an avid believer in the spirit world and regularly attended séances. Even when the most famous 'spiritualist' of the time, Margaret Fox, confessed it was all an act, Conan Doyle refused to believe her and even started giving public lectures on the subject. During one lecture, he was interrupted by a high-pitched whistle, which he took to be a sign from beyond the grave. It turned out to be the hearing aid of a member of the audience that needed its batteries changing.

Wacky works of art

The world's smallest painting

Don't be surprised if you never see the world's smallest painting. That's because *Fish*, created in 2007 by artist J Sha, is just 40 microns tall! That means it is smaller than a speck of dust and just 1/8th the width of a human hair. Pretty small, then. The artist created *Fish* using nanoentonography, a technique used by the makers of bank notes to prevent counterfeiting.

CrackPot Quiz Question

Q. What toy did the writer HG Wells play with all his life ...?

    a) toy soldiers;

    b) rubber duck;

    c) penny whistle.

The answer is a) toy soldiers. HG Wells (1866-1946), author of *The War of the Worlds* (1895), even wrote books on the subject. *Little Wars* (1913), is considered the definite rulebook for all future war gamers, so he wasn't wasting his time, at least!

1348	Black Death reaches Northern Europe
1390-1441	Jan van Eyck
1444-1510	Sandro Botticelli
1452-1519	Leonardo da Vinci
1471-1528	Albrecht Dürer
1492	**Columbus sails to America**
1519-1522	**Spanish expedition led by Magellan circumnavigates the globe**
1563	**Plague kills 80,000 people in England**
1571-1610	Michelangelo Merisi da Caravaggio
1666	**Great Fire of London**
1727-1788	Thomas Gainsborough
1775-1783	**American Revolutionary War**
1788-1824	Lord Byron
1789-1799	**French Revolution**
1812-1870	Charles Dickens
1819-1892	Walt Whitman
1828-1882	Dante Gabriel Rossetti
1832-1898	Lewis Carroll
1834-1903	James McNeill Whistler
1835-1910	Mark Twain
1837-1901	**Queen Victoria reigns over the British Empire**
1853-1890	Vincent van Gogh
1854-1900	Oscar Wilde

TIMELINE

	1859-1930	Arthur Conan Doyle
	1864	**Slavery abolished in the United States**
	1865	**President Abraham Lincoln assassinated**
	1874-1946	Gertrude Stein
	1881-1973	Pablo Picasso
	1882-1941	James Joyce
	1883-1924	Franz Kafka
	1886-1957	Diego Rivera
	1890-1976	Agatha Christie
	1891-1959	Stanley Spencer
	1892-1973	JRR Tolkien
	1896-1940	F Scott Fitzgerald
	1899-1961	Ernest Hemingway
	1904-1989	Salvador Dali
	1907-1954	Frida Kahlo
	1912-1956	Jackson Pollock
	1914-1997	William Burroughs
	1914-1918	**World War I**
	1917	**Russian Revolution**
	1922-1969	Jack Kerouac
	1923-2007	Marcel Marceau
	1928-1987	Andy Warhol
	1939-1945	**World War II**
	1969	**First man on the moon**

POLITE NOTICE: entries labelled with the patented 'pointy finger' signify noteworthy historical events - thank you.

Index